MW01530506

TABLE OF CONTENTS

Cover Art by
Matthew Archambault

Black & White Illustrations by
Ken Landgraf

EDCON
Publishing Group

Copyright © 2006
AV Concepts Corporation
Edcon Publishing Group

www.rempub.com

Printed in U.S.A.
ISBN# 1-55576-380-4

A MOUNTAIN IS TO CLIMB

Education.
Who needs it?

What a question to ask.
It's like asking, "What's
a mountain for?" and
being told that a
mountain is to climb.

Let's start by being honest
and admitting that no one
really needs an education.
Does that surprise you?

You could live your entire life
without ever learning how to
read.

Or how to write.

Chicken Salad
2 cups chicken, cubed
4 stalks celery, diced
1 diced onion
1 green pepper

A MOUNTAIN IS TO CLIMB

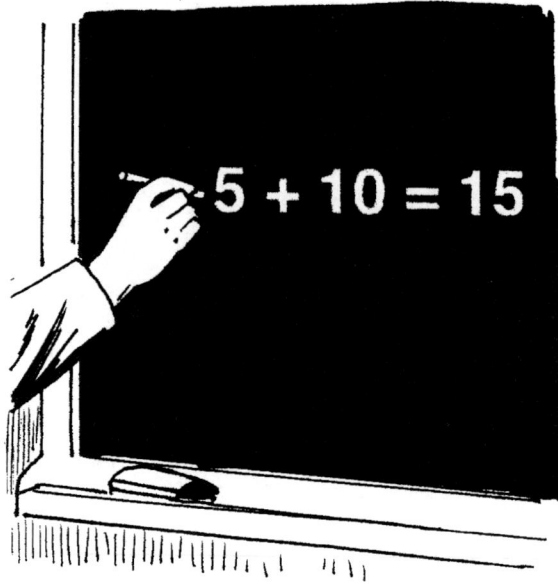

$$5 + 10 = 15$$

Or how to do math.

So we ask again, Who needs an education?
And we answer, maybe you do! Not just to live, but to live the kind of life you may want to live. But, perhaps you're already wondering if quitting school at age 16 would be the best thing for you to do. How can you decide?

A man named Harold Laswell studied people all over the world and found that there are eight things that all human beings want:

1. **Respect**
2. **Wealth**
3. **Power**
4. **Enlightenment**
5. **Skill**
6. **Justice & Fairness**
7. **Well-being**
8. **Affection**

Let's listen as a group of students discuss these universal values with their school counselor.

"I'd like to be respected very much. I'd like to have people respect my judgment and take me seriously," said Randy.

"I think respect is one of the most important things people need. I couldn't stand losing people's respect, because then I'd lose my self-respect. And self-respect is something that everyone needs," said Nora.

Okay. Respect seems to be something that most people desire. Can you respect yourself and get the kind of respect you want from others if you drop out of school?
Think about it. Without education, you could find yourself at the bottom of the mountain with everyone else looking down on you.

"Now what do you think about wealth as something to value?" asked the counselor.

A MOUNTAIN IS TO CLIMB

"Money isn't everything," said Derek.

"I don't want to be rich, and I don't want to be poor. I want to have a little more than normal. I'd like enough money to live comfortably – a nice house with a swimming pool – and to travel – and to take nice vacations at the shore."

Is there a relationship between getting a high school education and wealth? You'd better believe there is!

A MOUNTAIN IS TO CLIMB

Research shows that high school dropouts are frequently unemployed and on welfare. Among dropouts who get jobs, most are employed at low-skilled, low-pay work.

So money isn't everything, as Derek said, but low-skilled, low-pay jobs don't get you enough money for big houses, nice cars, vacations, and such.

Ask yourself, *do you really want to be poor?* If you decide to drop out of school, you will greatly increase the chance that you will spend the rest of your life in poverty at the bottom of the mountain!

Listen to the students' comments regarding power:

"Power is hard to get – but is needed to get to the top," said Tyrone. "I want to be the boss or the leader – not a follower."

Do you think a person needs an education to be a good leader? A person with very little education can get pushed around by others who use their knowledge and power to take advantage of people. Do you want to be powerless to defend yourself?

A MOUNTAIN IS TO CLIMB

"An enlightened person is one who wants to learn as much as possible. Why would this be important to us?" asked the counselor.

"I didn't know what enlightenment was, but now I think I'd like to have some."

The other students laughed at Bernadette's comment.

"Enlightenment is very important to me. I want the best education I can get!"

"Seriously," said Nora. "I'm willing to learn all I can. I admire people who are well educated."

"I'd like to learn more by traveling and meeting new people to develop my mind," said Randy.

❧   ❧

A mind is to develop, like a mountain is to climb.

A MOUNTAIN IS TO CLIMB

Still, there are millions of people so unenlightened or uneducated, that they cannot read or write well enough to properly complete a job application.

Remember, another hazard of being a dropout is being underemployed. Underemployment means having a lower level job than you are able to do. Is this what you want?

Who needs an education? Maybe you do.

"The fifth area of human value that people all over the world want is skill! How do you feel about skill as a value?"

"I'd like enough skill to be able to help my kids with their homework," said Randy.

Bernadette spoke next. "I'd like to be skillful so I can get a good-paying job – and that's important because most women work outside the home for at least 20 years."

"Being skillful about something would make me feel good about myself," said Derek.

Having skills will help you get a job and make you feel proud of yourself. If you drop out of school, both of these goals will be harder to reach.

"The sixth quality people want is justice and fairness."

"I'd like to have a fair chance in my life. My rights are very important to me," said Kim.

∾   ∾

If your rights are important to you, will you be able to stand up for them if you're poorly educated? Will you even know what your rights are?

Uneducated people find themselves at the bottom of the mountain, getting treated unfairly. Do you want to be one of them?

"The seventh quality of life all human beings want for themselves is well being – both physically and mentally," said the counselor.

"The more healthy you are, the longer you'll live," said Randy.

13

A MOUNTAIN IS TO CLIMB

"And the better you'll be able to handle the stressful situations of life without falling apart," added Derek.

To be healthy physically and mentally means that you know what to do and what not to do. Even health is related to education.

"The eighth and last quality of life that Laswell found all people desire is affection, or love. Any serious thoughts about this area?" asked the counselor.

"I'd like everybody to like me," said Randy.

"I'd want my wife to be able to get a good job," said Kim, "and not be a dropout. I wouldn't want her to be a quitter."

❧ ❧

Okay. Now it's your turn. We've shared with you, comments from other students about what they value. And now we invite you to think about what YOU value. Use Laswell's eight universal human values to help you think about your future life and the goals you want to reach.

You can set your goals low and live your whole life at the bottom of the mountain – or you can decide to climb higher up the mountain of life – but you'll need the proper tools and equipment to make that climb successful.

If you value living a life of quality, you'll need to be educated, since education is the equipment for success.

If you're in school today only because you're not yet old enough to quit, we offer you the challenge to begin to think about school in a new way – not as a place to get out of as soon as possible but, instead, as a place to equip yourself with the tools that are

Personal Development

It's your life and your future we're talking about – and only YOU can make the decision about what's important to you. Only YOU can climb to the top.

We hope you'll take our challenge to think about the quality of life YOU want to live. And we hope you'll make a wise decision – a decision to remain in school to supply yourself with the basic tools you'll need to reach the goals you want as you climb the mountain called life!

A MOUNTAIN IS TO CLIMB

A universal value is one that all people desire. Harold Laswell identified eight universal human values which are listed below. Rate each value and give a personal example. Try to add three additional values to the list.

VALUES	LOW	MEDIUM	HIGH	EXAMPLE
Respect				
Wealth				
Power				
Enlightenment				
Skill				
Justice/ Fairness				
Well-being				
Affection				
ADDITIONAL VALUES:				
1.				
2.				
3.				

Students who live with their parents or relatives often underestimate the amount of money they will need when they have to support themselves. There are two sides to every budget – income and expenses.

Income requires a job. Indicate the job you will have when you are finished with school, and your hourly wage.

Type of job: _____

Dollars per hour: _____

INCOME

Will you be able to get a full-time job? _____

Will you be able to get a part-time job? _____

How many hours will you work per week? _____

What will be your weekly paycheck after taxes are deducted?

_____

EXPENSES

Believe it or not, everyone gets sick.

What will one visit to the doctor cost? _____

What if you get a toothache? How much will it cost to see the dentist? _____

HOUSING

Rent _____

TRANSPORTATION

Bus or other public transportation _____

Automobile (estimated weekly expense for auto loan, insurance premium, gas and repairs) _____

FOOD

Breakfast _____   Lunch _____

Supper _____

Extra snacks & drinks _____

A MOUNTAIN IS TO CLIMB

List your weekly expenses.

Rent $ _____

Entertainment $ _____

Utilities (if not included) $ _____

Phone $ _____

Clothing $ _____

Savings $ _____

Miscellaneous $ _____

Total weekly expenses: $ _____

Total weekly income: $ _____

less (-)

Total weekly expenses: $ _____

                        = $ _____

Will you be able to live on your income? If not, you will have to make more money or reduce your spending plan.

Making more money requires a better job. Getting a better job requires a higher level of education.

Remember, the more you're in school and the more you learn… the more you'll earn!

A MOUNTAIN IS TO CLIMB

Personal Development

Sometimes students develop habits, attitudes, and behaviors that lead them to drop out of school. See how you rate by answering the following statements *TRUE* or *FALSE*.

TRUE (T) or FALSE (F)

_____1. I usually get into "trouble" by breaking a school rule or policy more than three times a year.

_____2. School activities, including sports, bore me, so I don't participate in anything.

_____3. I have always been a slow reader. I just don't like to read. I would rather watch T.V.

_____4. Sure, I know lots of kids, but I don't really have any friends at school.

_____5. My family will be glad when I leave home, and so will I.

_____6. If I don't feel like going to school, I don't go. I'm absent more than ten days a year.

SCORE

5-6 True - Probably will not finish high school. Are you sure this is what you want?

3-4 True - Borderline. You have a choice in finishing school.

1-2 True - You will make it. Congratulations!

THE PARTY

THE PARTY

"All right! That's more like it," said Rod as he revved up his motorcycle. "I know I can win the race when it runs like this."

"I hope so," said Rod's dad. "You've been working hard on that engine for days."

"Yeah," replied Rod. "I spent all yesterday afternoon cleaning the carburetor. That's why it sounds so sweet now."

"Yesterday afternoon?" questioned Rod's dad. "What about school?"

"Well...gee, Dad...so I didn't go. So what. I wouldn't have been ready for the race otherwise."

THE PARTY

"You may not be racing after all," scolded Rod's father. "School comes first, Rod. That affects your future. I'm really disappointed that you neglected your responsibility."

Rod became visibly upset. "What do you mean I might not be racing?"

"In order for you to race, you need my permission," replied Rod's dad. "I'll sign the form when your classwork is made up."

"Dad! No!" shouted Rod. "I won't have time before the race. I have to go to a birthday party tonight."

Rod's dad ignored his son's plea. "I'm sorry you chose not to take care of your responsibilities first."

"But, Dad!"

* * *

"Nice party, isn't it?" asked Janet. "I love the live music. Someday I'd like to sing with a group like Bill Zumbo's."

"They're good all right," said Rod. "I guess my mind really isn't on the party, though. I keep thinking about the race tomorrow. My dad won't let me enter the race."

"What!" said Janet with great surprise. "Why not? You've been looking forward to this race for weeks."

"I know," said Rod sadly. "I skipped school yesterday to work on my carburetor. And now my dad won't sign the permission form until I make up all of my work."

"What a drag," said Janet. "My mom's like that. School, school. Must get a good education and all that. That's all our parents ever think about. I'm going to sing with a rock group someday. Why do I need school?"

Just then Rod spotted Troy at the buffet table helping himself to some fruit. Troy was the older brother of his friend Dan. Troy worked at the Auto Body shop in town. "Let's go talk to him, Jan."

"Hi, guys," said Troy, as Rod and Janet approached the table. "Long time no see. What's new?"

THE PARTY

"Not much I guess," said Rod. "I can't be in the race tomorrow because I cut school yesterday. And my dad wants me to make up the work before I can race. Drag, huh?"

"Why did you cut out of school?" asked Troy.

"I needed time to clean my carburetor," answered Rod. "You know how important *that* is!"

"Sure do," said Troy. "That's important. But, it's not as important as being in school. If you think missing a race is a drag, you ought to try looking for a job when you don't have a high school education."

"Why, what do you mean? I never thought I'd hear that from you," said Rod.

"Well, a couple of years ago I would have been just like you and cut school to work on my bike. School was boring – and my parents were always nagging me about it. So, I decided to show them – I dropped out.

"I worked hard for places like Hamburger Heaven and Molly's Cleaning Service. Those were the only jobs I could get without an education.

"I tried to be Mr. Big Shot around my friends because I had a job and I didn't have to go to school. But, I wasn't really a part of things anymore. My friends kind of "tuned me out." After a while, I wised up and went back to school. But, when I started to register for classes, Mr. Davis talked me into taking Auto Body classes at the vocational high school. I did great – and I was prepared for a real job when I graduated."

"Auto Body? Hmmm," said Rod. "What other types of classes does the vocational school offer?"

Troy began to tell Rod all about the trade courses available at the vocational school. "There's Construction, Auto Repair, Food Services, Practical Nursing, Graphic Arts – all kinds of stuff."

"Don't they teach cosmetology, too?" asked Janet. "I thought I heard about that somewhere."

"How could I forget about that?" answered Troy. "That's the course my girlfriend took. She styles my hair for me. Well, it was good seeing both of you," said Troy, "but I must be going."

"Good-bye Troy," said Janet.

"See you later," said Rod.

*   *   *

THE PARTY

At the party, Janet spotted a familiar face. "Oh, there's Crissy," she said. "Over here, Crissy," she shouted.

"Hi," said Crissy, as she walked over to Janet and Rod. "Are you two a couple now?"

"Well, we just sort of ran into each other here," said Rod. "But, I'm taking Janet home tonight. If that's all right with you, Janet."

"Sure," smiled Janet. "How's that for a quick decision?" Then Janet asked Crissy, "What are you doing now, Crissy? I haven't seen you around school in a while."

"I dropped out about two months ago," Crissy answered. "I've been baby-sitting ever since. I'm going to school two nights a week now. And when I finish, I'm going to be a beautician. But, night school isn't free, and my parents are making *me* pay for it."

"Two nights a week?" said Janet. "Won't it take an awfully long time to complete the course that way?"

"Yes," sighed Crissy. "By the time I finish, the rest of you will have been out of school for almost a year. But, at least I won't have to spend the rest of my life baby-sitting."

"Crissy, I guess I don't understand why you don't just come back to school," said Janet.

"Well," Crissy began, "I didn't do much when I was in school. And I never did homework. I'm not sure that I would do any better now. Besides, I'm not part of the gang there anymore."

"How about just getting a GED and having it over with. Wouldn't that be simpler?" Janet asked.

"I know that works for some people," answered Crissy, "but I don't think I could pass the test. I'm not very good at math, and I really have trouble writing. Don't worry. I'm going to make it. Well, I have to go now. See ya."

When Crissy was out of sight, Janet turned to Rod. "You know, Rod, I used to think Crissy really had her head together, but baby-sitting all day?"

Just then Dave and Diana appeared. "Hi Dave, Diana," said Rod. "I haven't seen you two for a while. How's the world treating you?"

"Dave's celebrating," said Diana. "He just got offered an apprenticeship with The Blake Company. They accept high-school graduates with good work references, and they will guarantee him a job after six months of on-the-job training."

THE PARTY

"Way to go, Dave!" said Rod. "So, what will you be training to become?"

"An electrician," replied Dave. "I'll have some studying to do to learn the codes and stuff, but I think I'll like it."

"And electricians make good money," said Rod.

"Yeah," said Dave. "The first thing I'm going to do is sell my old motorcycle and buy some decent transportation."

"Let me know when you're ready to sell," said Rod.

"I will. But, you haven't heard Diana's news yet. She's finishing business school next month, and she's already lined up a secretarial job with The Blake Company."

Janet smiled. "So, you two will be able to take coffee breaks together."

"Right," replied Dave. "And in another year or so, we might be able to schedule vacation time together."

"That would be nice," said Rod.

"Let's leave these two lovebirds alone now," said Janet. "And congratulations to both of you."

Janet and Rod headed for the dance floor. After several dances, the band quieted down and Bill Zumbo grabbed the microphone. "Hey, is there a Janet Caldwell here tonight?" he asked.

Janet turned and faced the band. She raised her hand. "I'm Janet Caldwell," she said nervously.

Bill Zumbo smiled and walked over to Janet and Rod. "Hi, Janet," he said. "I'm Bill Zumbo. Your brother Rick told me about your interest in singing and he said to look for you here, tonight."

"Bill Zumbo! Wow!" said Janet, extending her hand for a handshake. "I just love your music. This is my friend Rod."

"Nice to meet you, Rod," said Bill, shaking Rod's hand.

"Hey, Janet," said Bill, "we're always looking for new talent. When will you be graduating?"

"In two more years," responded Janet. "But, what does graduating have to do with singing?"

"That's a good question," said Bill. "The fact is that it takes more than talent and good looks to make it in the music business. You need common sense, a lot of drive, and a little bit of luck doesn't hurt either.

"You know, finishing high school is an achievement, and knowing that you have achieved gives you the confidence to keep on achieving.

"And, maybe just as important is the fact that when you finish high school, you give yourself a door you can open to all sorts of jobs.

"All of us in the band have other jobs that we go back to from time to time. We love playing together, but when the music business doesn't go well, we still have to live."

Janet said, "Gosh. I thought as well-known as you all are, you wouldn't need other jobs."

THE PARTY

Bill laughed. "Most people think that. Anyway, I'd like to hear from you after you graduate. If you're still interested in singing at that time, look me up."

"Thanks, Bill," said Janet. "You bet I will."

When Bill walked away, Janet asked Rod, "Would you mind taking me home now, Rod? I have some things I need to think about."

"Of course," said Rod. "I do too. I just hope I can get my make-up work done in time to get some sleep before the race."

THE PARTY

SCHOOL IMPROVEMENT

Often, students can make suggestions on ways to improve their school. This makes learning easier. See if you can come up with at least five (5) ways you could improve your school.

1. _____

   _____

   _____

2. _____

   _____

   _____

3. _____

   _____

   _____

4. _____

   _____

   _____

5. _____

   _____

   _____

THE PARTY

Many students are headed on a career track; others would rather learn a trade. Indicate the subjects that you might like to study by checking the appropriate line.

Place a √ on the appropriate line.

	Low Interest	High Interest
Auto Body Repair	_____	_____
Auto Mechanics	_____	_____
Business/Accounting	_____	_____
Carpentry	_____	_____
Computer Programming	_____	_____
Cosmetology	_____	_____
Child Care	_____	_____
Drafting and Design	_____	_____
Electronics	_____	_____
Electrician	_____	_____
Fashion Design	_____	_____
Graphic Arts	_____	_____
Horticulture (plants)	_____	_____
Law Enforcement	_____	_____
Marketing and Sales	_____	_____
Masonry/Tile Setting	_____	_____
Machine Shop	_____	_____
Medical/Nursing	_____	_____
Photography	_____	_____
Plumbing/Pipe Setting	_____	_____
Sewing/Textile	_____	_____
Sheet Metal	_____	_____
Systems Analysis	_____	_____
Welding	_____	_____